Silence

is

Broken

By Jacqueline Robinson

Published by Jewelmark Press 2009

All Bible quotes are from the King James Bible

A CIP record for this book is available from the British Library

ISBN 978-0-9562727-0-6

Cover Design by Marie Reid

Jewelmark butterfly image Copyright © 2003 Gill Carter

I dedicate this book to David, Victoria, Jewel, Asore, Sashenie, Sheron, Cheryl and Tyrone

Who have loved me unconditionally

Acknowledgements

I would like to thank all those who have encouraged me through the journey of writing this book. I have appreciated all the feedback I have received.

I would however, like to give special thanks to the following friends: Victoria Robinson, Sheron Watson, Tyrone Watson, Andrea Carnegie, Kevin Bevas, Antoinette Eccleston-Deslandes, Mark Bennett and Cheryl Folkes.

Finally, I am truly grateful to all those who have inspired me to write along the way.

Forward

Most of us live our everyday lives at an unsustainable speed and propensity. For some it is a self imposed velocity caused by over crammed diaries and overloaded itineraries, whilst for others it is a mere consequence of post-modern living. Technology and the internet have improved communications and brought us all closer together 'virtually', but the speed at which we whizz by on a text message, email or face-book message begs me to ask, are we any closer socially, emotionally, spiritually?

The poems in this book press pause on our fast-forward society. In doing so, with choice words they present images, pictures and people you may have missed on your way to the next appointment. They give a microphone to the real voices behind easy to assume stereotypes, and amplify the unsaid meanings hiding in polite conversation.

My advice to you would be, not to rush through this book, but to take the time to perceive and not just see, feel and not just touch, listen and not just hear the sounds that emerge when our silences are finally broken.

Andrea Carnegie

Introduction

The Silence Is Broken is a collection of poems which express the silent thoughts that we carry within us. The poems reflect a variety of experiences and have been inspired both by conversations the author has had with individuals, quiet meditation and prayer.

The direct language used transports the reader to the very heart of the ordeal leaving them with a very real sense of what is being felt.

The book is in four sections:

Hooked – describes the emotions of those trapped by their position, thoughts or substance addiction.

Damaged – describes a variety of situations which have left a profound emotional scar on the individuals involved. This section recognises there are many people living with these scars that can relate personally to what is being said but never describe what they are feeling.

Challenged – presents a view that may confront the reader's status quo and shift them from a place of comfort.

Loved – expresses the author's feelings to those closest to her.

The Silence Is Broken is a book not only to be read but experienced.

Contents

LOVED

HOOKED

My Love

For richer, for poorer
In sickness and in health
I'll never leave you
Many have told me to give you up
But I have vowed to be with you
Until death us do part

I love your bronze and golden tones
And your inner strength
I love when you're transparent
You make me feel good about myself
And life in general
I'll never leave you

Some say you'll only destroy me
They tell me I've changed
Since I married you
You don't have my best interests at heart
I've lost friends because of you
I've lost the respect of others
Because of you

But my love for you is so powerful
That it doesn't matter
Who needs them anyway?

Together we can face the world
My dearest RUM – I'll never leave you

The Crack Screen

The crack screen
Separates me from myself
The self that hurts
I value the time
Even though it's a moment
Ten minutes of flight – anesthetised

I'm being sucked down
Slowly down into the whirlpool
Of my inner mind
Past pain and present turmoil
Swirling around together
Going round and round

I have to
Crave to
Rush back behind the screen
What can I do?
Where?
Who?
How?
When?

I need the screen to protect
Myself from my self

Weed

"Give me the weed, the good Ganja weed" you cry
Since when has weed been good?
It entangles and strangles the life out of
Everything in its way
Including you

Drawing the draw
You believe the lie that you are wise
And full of overstanding
Not recognising that the Babylon
You are trying to escape
Is in fact
Your mind

Higher heights and deeper depths you seek
An alternative outlook of the world
Clouding your views with the smoke of deception

No smoking here
The view is clear
And I can see Captive
You are enslaved by your addiction

The Trip

Excited – I've fastened my seat belt,
I'm ready to fly
I'm about to depart
Clutching my valium

Pop – I'm now relaxed
I've made this trip many times
Departure point – Unhappiness
Soaring towards elation I feel free

Truth – I'm taking a trip
But not travelling anywhere
Why don't I ever arrive at my true destination
Happiness
I'm pursuing liberty
But know I'm bound
God help me!

The Record

From bong to mong
Same old song
Scratched
Stuck on the groove
Round and round
Can't escape
Please somebody
Lift the needle

Trapped

I'm trapped by my thoughts about myself
Don't you understand?
I can't just go out there and do something
There's always someone so much better
I'm destined to be a failure
I'm just not good enough – a letdown

I'm trapped by my thoughts about myself
Why don't you get it?
Black clothes always hide me
I can't wear colourful clothes
They will highlight the fact
That there are others who are
Prettier than me
Slimmer than me
Fatter than me
I'm just not good enough – a letdown

I'm trapped by my thoughts about myself
Why are you asking me why?
I'm so grateful
That he has chosen to be with me
So what if he calls me names and hits me
Now and then

I probably deserve it
I'm just not good enough – a letdown

Trapped by my thoughts about myself
Can't you see?
It's my fault I'm in a childless marriage
It's because of my infertility
Everyone has the right to call me barren or a mule
Both to my face and behind my back
I'm just not good enough – a letdown

Trapped by my thoughts about myself
You are so dumb
Me minister
What can I do?
God can't use me
I'm just not good enough – a letdown

Guaranteed Love

After meeting you it didn't take long
Before I know you were to be my wife
My queen
I loved your smile, your voice
Your skin, your touch
My whole being came alive
Just at the thought of you

You grew to love me with such intensity
My strength and vulnerability
I knew you would love me through
My triumphs and failures
Totally guaranteed
Or so I thought

As the years went on
I felt comfortable with our union
But with routine, comes monotony
And boredom at times
I began thrill seeking
I craved an adrenaline rush
Wanting to constantly try something new
Someone different
It's nothing, no one serious
It's just a game

I became a player

But I knew your adoration
Respect and care
Through my triumph and failures
Were totally guaranteed
Or so I thought

I didn't hear your pleas for us to
Spend more time together
I didn't see the distance grow between us
I was a player and loving it
I felt invincible
I wasn't going to let you
Take that away from me
Drag me back to the routine

But one day
You spoke words I hadn't heard before
You don't love me anymore
You're leaving
You want a divorce

Now, I'm left alone
Facing my biggest failure
Without the guarantee
Of your total love

I'm More Than Just a Rug

As caregiver to all
I'm left with just the dregs of time
For myself
I dare not think about chasing my own
Dreams anymore
Experience has taught me that
The daily pressures I face will cause them
To evaporate into a mist

My darling husband
I know you love me so much
But you rarely acknowledge
That I am constantly overstretched
I juggle your needs with that of
Our children and parents
Sometimes I think you are blind
To my tiredness
You seem unable to sense my weariness
You speak words of support
But your actions say
'Just get on with it and stop moaning'

When I look in the mirror
I no longer see a self that I recognise
The career – pursuing

Fun loving person I was
Has been distorted
The reflected image is of one
Who is slowly being compressed
Into a bitter but depressed super woman
Who is unable to satisfy her own needs
Because of the never ending demands
Of others

My sweetheart
Why do my cries for help fall on deaf ears
Why can't we have an equal share
Of the load
I know you are competent
And are concerned about
The needs of others
What about mine?
Or is this your twisted way of controlling what I do
And who I see?

You are and always will be
The love of my life
But right now I'm on an endless carousel of
Negative emotions
There are days when all I want to do
Is curl up and cry

And others where I have serious thoughts of
Packing my things
And running away

I'm sad and ashamed to admit
To the days where I think of ways to end my life
Pills and alcohol
Cutting
Hanging
I've considered them all
Just to escape

Don't get me wrong
I want to care for my loved ones
Just give me some space

As caregiver to all
I often feel taken for granted
Especially by you
Please don't push me over the edge

I decide how much I give
Not you
My place is not under your feet
I'm more than just a rug
For you to use and abuse

It's Time

It's time my flower
To come out of the shade
To embrace the sunshine
Experience rejuvenation
And the liberty it brings

It's time my flower
To come out of the shade
Enjoy each raindrop
As it washes away
The grime accumulated
Whilst living in the shade

It's time my flower
To come out of the shade
To unfurl your petals
To allow your sweet
Fragrance to once again
Profusely enter into areas
You have never been

It's time my flower
To come out of the shade
To grow strong
To expose yourself

To a new life
New experiences

It's time my flower
For me to tell you that you are
Significantly beautiful
You bring infinite pleasure
You have been so generous
By sharing your exquisiteness with me
I truly appreciate every aspect of you
I can't imagine life
If the vase was empty
And you were not there

DAMAGED

Adultery

With your first act of adultery
You ripped my heart out
The pain was so harsh, it burned like fire
I was anesthetised
To all other aspects of life
I thought the only pain I would bear
Because of you was in labour
I gladly suffered – our children are beautiful

Flashback.....
I remember how we climbed
To the pinnacle of love
Constantly driven by passion
Constantly interlocked
Now, I close my eyes
Because I don't want to see you
I can't face you
Now, I'm giddy from questions
Racing around in my mind
How could you? Why? When?
How often? How long?
How safe?
G.U.M.????????

They say time is a healer
But you have used time
To develop your skill
As an adulterer
A free flow of lies
To me and them

You have stamped on my heart
Over and over again
Flattened, squash, squelch
You don't hear the sound
But you wonder why I'm heartless

"Create in me a clean heart, and renew a right
spirit in me"
Psalm 51:10

Rejection

I did it all
Everything I was taught to do
I worked hard to provide for my family
I gave up socialising every night with
My friends
I stayed at home
Showering her with love
She had my full attention

Suddenly she said I was boring
Stuck in a routine
She said she wanted more excitement and fun
She accused me of having a deep relationship
With the tv remote
She said I needed to find my purpose
Outside interests

My daily work is a constant fight
To reach targets, be the best
Meet objectives

When I come home, it's a haven
A place where I can be myself
A place I expect to unwind
A place I expect to be loved

Disbelief
I'm stunned
She says she's found someone else
She's fed up of me
I'm dull

I feel as if I have been dealt
A knock out blow
I'm floored……
I didn't see it coming

Never again
I'll never allow any woman
To get close to my heart
My guard is up
Now, I'm pulling the punches

The Player

Beware of the player
Oh yes you say
I know his game
He travels without a care
Laying down
No roots
Spreading his seed liberally

Not him I say
I mean
The player who never deposits anything
The player who never seeks
Your hidden chambers
One who plays an intricate game of manipulation
Always interested
Attentive to every detail
Every compliment carefully chosen
Gently placing his hand on the small of your back

He's not a player you say
He's not just flirting
He's genuine
This relationship will grow
Will go somewhere

But he does this with every woman
Simultaneously
You are no more special than the others
He brings you to the point where you think
He'll commit
But he never does

What does he get in return?
Access to clothes, money, time and food
All at no cost to him
Coming in from different routes
Different sources
There's no two timing as he's never
Committed to anyone
Everyone's a target to be used
He can make a swift get away
When she cottons on to the fact
That she will never receive something tangible

But what does he really want I ask
His orgasmic thrill comes
From the knowledge that he is
Desperately wanted
He feels validated and accepted

I Don't Get It

Why do you play?
Why do you have that incessant need to conquer?
Why do you need to hear
That you're the greatest lover?
Why do my orgasms mean more to you
Than they do to me?
Why are you competing with the unseen
The unknown?
Why do you think that my body belongs to you?

The Truth
Two can play
I'm never conquered
Every one is the greatest lover
They are not always real
No one cares if you win
You only have what I give

But hey, I know you can't handle the truth

Stand

You are a man
Designed by God to stand
To work
To provide
To lead
To protect
To love
To cherish
You have chosen not to live your life this way
Together forever
I think not
What's the use
If all you can do is stand

The Job

We meet
We chat
You smile

You hold my hand
But I can't feel it
You kiss my lips
But nothing ignites
You caress my body
But my senses are dull
You roam inside.....
Looking?
But can't find me

I'm not there
It's just a job
If you want to find ME
I'm over there in the bottle

Counterfeit Love

Yes at last I've found the real deal
You are thoughtful and considerate
You treat me like a queen
You say all the things I want to hear
Although you are clearly strong
You treat me with a gentleness
Unfamiliar to me

You're almost too good to be true

You've conquered my mistrust
I'm now free to reveal my true self
I dance in the rain of your declared love
All inhibitions abandoned
I'm ready to give you my all
The voices of caution in my head
Are a distant whisper
You were meant for me

This feeling is too good to be true

I declare to the world
Our union is permanent
I stare at flowers, dresses and cakes
Multiple plans whizzing around my head

Colour themes, cars, venues
So many decisions to make

When questioned
I ask for a platinum ring with
Princess Cut diamonds
It looks magnificent on my finger
The sparkle of success

Another ring for my collection
I've played the game well
I'm getting better every time
Counterfeit love
I'm gonna screw you
Before you screw me!

Your Sentence

My sentence
When spoken takes up a few seconds
I often don't remember the sentences I speak
There are so many throughout a day

You spoke a sentence
Which threw my life into chaos
Removed my daily freedom for 20 months
And caused me not to be able to travel abroad
For a further year

Your words separated me
From my children
And turned my parent's life upside down
They caused my husband to cry rivers of tears

As your sentence dawned on me
I became suspended in time
Paralysed by shock
Dumbstruck

I waited for you to speak another sentence
Cancelling the previous one
You didn't say another word
No more sentences
You just left me with a sentence

Invisible

I see the white van
Memories race back to my mind
Locked in a metal coffin
Unable to alter my position
Unable to move
All emotion drained from my frame
Leaving just a shadow behind

I observe people through
Orange tinted glass
No idea of where I'm going
Life continues as normal for the world
Whilst my world has been crushed to dust
I'm invisible
No one knows I'm here
They can't see me anymore

Too exhausted to keep looking
I turn to my company
A stale cheese sandwich and water
My induction into a system designed
To penalise me at every opportunity
Remove my fighting spirit and
Reduce me by force to a clone

As the van passes
I think of those inside

Life

You cross from liberty to death
I cross from liberty to life
All it took was one long outward breath

If only you could inhale again
All would be restored to its former state

Now my life is contained in a room
With a few possessions
I do it up the best I can
Whilst your life
Is in another's room
Marked by a few possessions

I seek solace in the arms of a mirror image
The years drag on
I'm a shadow of my former self
Friends come and go
Like waves on a beach
No one constant

I parent through visits
The phone and letters
Hoping my children will truly understand
Why they were not in the midst
Of my thoughts
When you crossed from liberty to death
And I crossed from liberty to life

59 Minutes

59 minutes until you lift the flap to see if
I'm in this world or the next
59 minutes to reflect.....
I think of my son. Your last night I partied
On drink and drugs
I came home too tired
To understand your cry
Son I'm sorry I didn't hear your cry for help
I thought you were a bit off colour
A temperature perhaps
I didn't know your heart was sick and that
You were going to die
I was too mashed to listen to your cry

59 minutes to remember our last Christmas Dad
When I told you
I hated you and wished you were dead
I didn't expect you to make
That wish come true
I didn't get a chance to say sorry
I didn't mean it
How many pills did you take?
59 minutes to consider how low I made
You feel
How I crushed you

Even if you don't blame me Mum does
You were the best Dad I had
I can't count my real Dad as real Dads
Don't do those things to their children

59 minutes to remember the unspeakable things
The stuff I don't talk about
Why didn't Mum believe me?
Why couldn't she accept the truth?

59 minutes to mull over how much Mum hates me

In the next 59 minutes
I will dream about how to end my life
I can't see any reason for continuing.
What have I to look forward to......
Another day in prison
Can I face another day of them lifting the flap
Every 60 minutes?

What's my life worth anyway?

POETRY LIBRARY

Just a Simple Hair Cut

She thought it was just a simple hair cut
But as each strand of her hair
Fell to the ground
She slowly became detached
From her anger

The rage that caused her
To destroy her environment
And feel vindicated
The fury which gripped her like a typhoon
Tossed her about like a scrap of paper
Out of control
The pain that was slowly
Strangling her destiny
Leaving her so vulnerable

The more hair that came off
The more liberated she felt
Cut free from the old chains of bondage
Free to be a new person
Behave in a different way
Free to be at peace
Open to love and be loved

As new hair grows
She feels empowered to decide
Her purpose
Fulfil her dreams
As she styles her hair
She shapes her prospects
She thought it was a simple hair cut
But it was the beginning of
An unsullied future

Hello

I browse the shop shelves
You say "excuse me"
I turn, it's You
We are polite and exchange "Hello"
You move on

Your "Hello" picked the scab concealing
The memories of our time together
The raw pain exposed
Our history of shared
Disappointment, distress
Hurt, sadness and longing
I want to find a corner and just weep
I'm surrounded by shoppers who can't see
My inner turmoil
I'm isolated....
Next time I see you
I won't say "Hello"

The Streatham Strip

As I walk along the Streatham Strip
Looking for the next john
You judge and scorn my empty shell
Not realising that we both trade our bodies for
Cash or its equivalent
The difference is
You try to call it a relationship
Even though it's loveless
We're both just going through the motions

When you look at me
Undressed
Do you see yourself?
A woman who deserves to be loved?
A woman who deserves to be cared for?
What makes you think that
We are so dissimilar to each other?

When I look at me
I see a woman who has been
Systematically raped
By life's experiences and circumstances
Leaving a total loss of self respect, self esteem.....
In fact a total loss of self

When you look at you
What do you see?
I'm telling you sister
When I look at you
I see me

Protection

Oh Mother
You have the instinct of a lion
When it comes to protecting your child
Ready to attack anyone who
May threaten or harm

As you walk in the sun
You ensure that your child
Is shielded from its fierce rays
Your child's delicate skin preserved
Your love is clear to see

Why, then Oh Mother
Do you bathe your child in expletives?
Why do you describe one so dependent
And vulnerable as a little ******?

You expect so much from your young one
You assume your child will develop thick skin
You leave them to guess
That you don't really mean it
You suppose your child will learn
That love that sounds like hate is really love
When your child becomes an adult
How will they recognise love?

How will they identify protection?
How will they measure their self worth?

I wonder to myself Mother about your
Ability to truly safeguard
And why for your child's sake
You didn't use protection

We All Have Issues

We all have issues
Or our issues have us?
She lived with her issue for twelve years
It constantly drained her
Causing her life to slip away drop by drop
She was unable to be herself
Amongst others
Always on her guard
Always on the look out
Worried her secret issue may show
She tried hard to conceal it

Recognising her vulnerability
She sought professional help over and over again
She sacrificed her financial stability
Seeking a cure, searching for liberty
But her trust was rewarded with
Manipulation and exploitation
Her issue left her a social reject

But one day, she decided to trust
One more person
Having a strong belief that one touch
Would free her from her issue

She didn't care about
The people around her
She was determined to reach out
She was changed
In an instant
Her issue was gone

Her faith touched Him to the core
He felt different because of it

Where are we?
Are we clutching our issues
Like a comfort blanket
Too afraid of life without them?
Are we happy to let our issues
Determine who we trust
And how we interact
With those around us?
Are we covering up our issues
With a fake smile,
Secretly unwilling to truly connect
With anyone?
Blind to the fact
That a life of freedom is slipping away

Deal your issues a blow
Reach out, believe and touch Christ
He can and will free you from them

Let both of you feel the Change

Luke 8:43-48

Oh Earthly Shepherd

Oh Earthly Shepherd
Where are you?
I'm lost and feel very alone
I'm constantly listening for your voice
A call, a text, an email, a visit

I speculate about whether you have noticed
That I'm missing
So busy, always busy
I assume looking after the other 99.....
Now I'm not sure

Oh Earthly Shepherd
Where are you?
I'm lost and feel very alone
I'm constantly listening for your voice
A call, a text, an email, a visit

I have wondered and wandered
Into unchartered territory
The terrain of my circumstances are unfamiliar
I'm unclear of how to handle this situation
I can't see an exit

Oh Earthly Shepherd
Where are you?
I'm lost and feel very alone
I'm constantly listening for your voice
A call, a text, an email, a visit

My desire to pray has vanished
My desperation and hopelessness
Has stemmed the flow of my praise
I don't know what to do

Oh Earthly Shepherd
Where are you?
I'm lost and feel very alone
I'm constantly listening for your voice
A call, a text, an email, a visit

I can't see my way out
My sight is obscured
By the constant stream of tears
I'm gripped by fear

Oh Earthly Shepherd
Where are you?
I'm lost and feel very alone

I've got to the point now
Where I'm no longer expecting you
You have proved that
You only pretend to care
When you can see me
I feel so low

Oh Earthly Man
(Cause you're not my shepherd)
Really and truly – where are you?
Anyway, it doesn't matter anymore
Frankly, I don't give a fig

Not only do I feel lost
But now I feel abandoned
The difference for me is
This is now my new habitat

I still remain
Astounded, by the fact
You couldn't find the time to give me
A call, a text, an email, or a visit

CHALLENGED

Mandate

You are a Man
With a clear mandate from God
Prosper, reproduce, subdue
Take charge, be responsible
Can you rise to the challenge?
You already have within you the things you need
Patience, grit, wisdom, tenacity amongst others

You are a Man
With a clear mandate from God – to love
Loving god first, yourself and your neighbour third
Giving Him the first fruits of your love is
Sometimes easier
Than loving yourself
Wrapped up in the definition of yourself
Is your wife
As you have become one
But He has already catered
For all your needs
He has already met all the deficits
You were born with
So just love without reservation
You are a Man
With a clear mandate from God
To spread the Good News of salvation

Through Jesus
This I know is your greatest challenge
Vulnerability and submission
Of your will to His own
Is an uncomfortable place for you
Having your own life transformed
By the Holy Spirit
In order to be a vessel
To transform others lives is
Full of unpredictability
I know you don't like that

But this awesome, all mighty, all powerful God
Trusts you
Has chosen you
To be His eyes, His ears, His hands
And so my brother, not only do I love you
But I trust you
Man of God

Circumcised Lips

Circumcised lips speak cleansing words
They declare God's judgement
They reveal God's plan and purposes
They pronounce life into dead situations
They affirm God's truth

Circumcised lips demonstrate
What happens when we are
Obedient at the optimal time
They are able to speak with
Divine authority and power
Transforming lives
Connecting people with God

Circumcised lips reflect
A lifestyle governed by the Word of God
That Word has pared away
The fleshly output of the mouth
The lies, deceit, and flattery
Which mask truth

Circumcision is painful
It demands self sacrifice
And can leave us feeling
Vulnerable and exposed

It leads to the difficulty of constant
Self appraisal to keep in line with His move
A daily realignment of our will to His

Circumcised lips
Have entered an agreement
To speak, to pray, to sing
On the Master's behalf
And in return reap a renewed mind
Which is not self serving
Defined by ambition
But defined by humility and submission

What Are You Bringing to His House?

What are you bringing to His house?
How valuable is it?
He measures the value of your tribute
By your level of sacrifice and
Your willingness to contribute
Small portions can equal large
If the quality is the same
Let us be careful not to give from a residual pot
The leftovers, the dross
Be open handed

What can I bring – I hear you ask?
Skills, money, time, talents, things
All types of resources are important to Him
Look into your heart and seriously consider
All you have to present
Let your giving be determined by the
Quiet voice of His Spirit
Not by what your eyes and ears
Know of what others are doing

Acknowledge
That He knows all of your gifts
He has provided all of your resources
He is waiting to use our offerings
To build a Kingdom for His glory

Exodus 35-36:6

Breakout

What exactly are you waiting for?
You know your spiritual gift

Our Father has graciously entrusted you
With a special gift
A special responsibility

If I had given you a wrapped present
You would have no hesitation
In tearing off the paper to explore what's inside

What exactly are you waiting for?
You know your spiritual gift

Is it for someone else to tell you
What your gift is?
Why?
The Holy Spirit has already told you
And confirmed it over and over again

What exactly are you waiting for?

Breakout of the limitations
Placed on you by others
Smash through the wall

Of low confidence and fear
Liberty and freedom are on the other side
Lives are waiting to be changed

Get familiar with your gift
Allow it to flow through your everyday life
Constantly honouring God

Breakout, Breakout, Breakout!

What exactly are you waiting for?
You know your spiritual gift

How long exactly do you expect to retain This gift
Whilst doing nothing
This is serious

Breakout

Grace

What is the colour of Grace?
Is it blood red?
Emerging from the sacrifice
Christ made at Calvary
Offering us cleansing
Affording us protection

What is the colour of Grace?
Is it sunshine yellow?
Illuminating our mind
Melting the icy consequences of sin
Radiating through us
Converted to kind actions towards others

What is the colour of Grace?
Is it heavenly blue?
Sanctifying us
Enabling God to dwell in us
Allowing us to converse with Him
And participate in the execution of His will

Whatever the colour of Grace
I am so glad that God has blessed
Me with his unmerited favour
My gratitude will last throughout eternity

Definition

We are comfortable with
How we define ourselves
Friend of God, His sons and daughters
Disciple of Christ
These all of course are all true
I'm eternally grateful for the
Grace which has facilitated this

But does this new definition
Give us the right
To define others by their sin
Homosexual, prostitute
Fornicator, murderer
We sometimes say these words
With so much scorn
None of us are
The personification of our sin
In fact, none of us are sinless
But yet we conveniently forget
The love of Christ
The very thing which redefined us
Is what we are called to show to everyone
Especially those who have not yet met with or
Submitted to our Master

We have a responsibility to be the mirror
Image of that love at every opportunity

Part of our definition is to be
The salt and light to the world
Let us recognise and live up to the fact
That we are the only
Christ some people meet

What is Your Position?

What is your position when you're in the furnace?
Are you crouched in the corner?
Gripped by fear
Convinced you're going to burn
Waiting for what you think is the inevitable

Are you kneeling?
Partially broken by disillusionment
Shaking an angry fist at God
Forgetting past victories
Consumed by the 'now' hurt and despair

Or are you standing tall?
With arms raised in surrender
Thanking God for His divine plan
And higher thoughts
Praising God because you expect the miraculous

If you continue to stand
You'll notice
That although the flames are intense
The situation looks dim
You are OK – you're not burning
He IS sustaining you
You're being refined

Black Rose

Beautiful, delicate Black Rose
You say .....
You're not as red as a poppy
You're not as fragrant as a lilly
You're not as open as a germini
You're not a vibrant as a daffodil
You're not a tall as a sunflower

We all have imperfections
But dear flower
None of these detract from your unique
And stunning shapeliness
Neither do they take
Anything away from your impact

When I look at you
I see pure and simple elegance
You may feel vulnerable at times
But I see your strength
You have withstood a variety of elements
Enabling me to have the opportunity
To derive immense pleasure
From gazing at you
Touching you
Smelling you

Your presence is awesome
Ultimately, we both know
You are 'good' in His sight

Single

Don't feel sorry for me
Because I am single
I am enjoying all that life has to offer
I have chosen this path
It's not that I have not been chosen

I do not need a husband
To validate my existence
Or to endorse my decisions
And although I love children
I do not need to have my own
In order for me to feel a sense of purpose

I am often judged
And sometimes condemned
For not pursuing single men
In the same manner a greyhound
Pursues the bunny
On a race track

I am content in my belief
That God created me in His own image
A whole person

He has positioned me in a world
With so much to discover
So much to enjoy
Placed within me so much to give

So let me get on with doing just that
Save your pity for someone who really needs it.

My Hair

When you look at me
You only see my hair
As you look at each lock
You attempt to classify
My religious affiliation
My ideological position
You reconfigure me to
Squeeze into your predefined
Assumptions

But I define myself
As a child of God
Walking daily with Christ alone
My ideology is purely that
Which is presented in the Word of God
I am seeking only to do the
Will of the Father
And to fulfil His divine purpose for my life

When you look past my hair
You'll see me

The Cost

What is the cost of being married to you?

The average wedding now costs 20k
Then there's the cost of a new car, clothes
And the general maintenance of a wife
We won't even talk about the cost
Of having and supporting children
Up to and throughout adulthood

But those costs are not the ones
That concern me most

Will you enhance or diminish my ministry?
Will we build up each other in Christ or
Will you cause me to lose my salvation?
I'm giving you my reputable name
Will you add value to it or destroy it?
Will you drain me emotionally to the point
That I can't give to those in need?

Will you cause men to commend my judgement
Because I have chosen a wife of integrity
Honour and virtue
Or will they just think I'm a mug?

What is the true cost of being married to you?

What is Under Your Wedding Dress?

My Bride
What is under your wedding dress
So white, pure and spotless?
A satin teddy, silk stockings?
Untouched territories
Waiting for exploration

Under my wedding dress you ask?
There lies my nakedness
I refer to the part of me that
You can't see
You can't touch
You can't hold

My vulnerability
My indecisiveness
My unspoken thoughts
My fears

Please don't touch my dress
As much as I love you
I'm not sure if I'm ready
To stand naked before you
I'm unsure you'll still love me
If you see me naked

Don't question me!
Don't pressure me!
I'm well aware you have waited a lifetime
For this moment
But I will undress in my own time
No amount of cajoling
Will change my mind
I feel I have too much to lose if I rush
I dread being left wanting more
Than you have to offer right now

My Groom
Stop and think for a minute
Are you truly prepared to stand
In front of me naked?
Everything I previously saw uncovered
Stripped of the image you presented
Your vulnerability
Your indecisiveness
Your unspoken words
Your fears
Exposed
For me to scrutinise
Criticise
Ridicule
Dismiss
Mmmmm

Your silence is audible

What's under my wedding dress you ask?
A desire to move trust to a new level
A desire to create a union
Where we feel safe
To reveal all to each other
A passion to be intimate with you
But on every possible level

The Bride

Oh Bride of Christ
Your face looks picture perfect
Your dove-like eyes
Have seen the salvation of the Lord
Your nose has smelt
The heady fragrance of pure sacrifices to God
You have tasted the sweetness of the Word

Your bridal dress is brilliant white
Ornately decorated
With precious jewels, sequins and beads
Representing your chastity, virtue and integrity

But why Christ Bride is your skirt raised so high
Exposing your secret chambers
I notice your gospel clad legs
Are full of pus-ridden scabby sores
On closer examination I see writing
Within each one

Malice, unforgiveness, disobedience, envy
Lying, jealousy, pride to name a few
All oozing a bloody mix of pus and water
Threatening to soil your dress

As I stand watching
I witness your surrender
As the cold finger of idolatry
Traces your vulva

STOP!!!

WHAT IS WRONG WITH YOU!!!!

Wake up Christ Bride
You can't afford to be
Mesmerised or persuaded
To relinquish your virgin state
This dalliance will surely end in your death

Remember how much your Bridegroom loves you
Remember how much He was willing to sacrifice
Just to have you as His Bride
Remember the passion
You have for your Lord

Stop picking your sores
With the nails of continuous sin
Healing is swift
When you apply grace
Mingled with His blood

You can, if you repent NOW
Be restored to your original beauty

An unsullied Bride in an unstained dress
That's what He's returning for

THINK ABOUT WHAT YOU ARE DOING
Live to honour your Bridegroom

What's Happened?

You say you've come to see me
You've come to spend time with me
Listen to me
Commune with me
What did you bring?
What have you got with you?

You have brought a smile for just a few
Gossip for your friends
Then there's the anger
And cross words for the others

You have come to my sanctuary
But where is your worship
You've lost your praise
You're happy to watch others
Exalt my name
With a sealed mouth
And a closed heart

You have allowed sin and idols
To crawl all over your life like
An infestation of cockroaches
Emerging from the
Dark secret places within

The truth is my child
That nothing is ever hidden from me
I see and know all things

But as I remember the sacrifice
My Son made
Grace is flowing continually
From me to you
I am waiting
To embrace you
To purge you
To restore you
I have a plan and purpose for your life
Come walk with me

Listen

Listen to me
Just listen
Stop talking
Stop asking
Stop pleading
Stop crying
Stop singing
Just be still

Listen to me
Just listen
Stop telling me how to talk to you
Stop telling me when to talk to you
Stop telling me what to talk about
Just be still

Listen to me
Just listen
I'm speaking when you read my word
I'm speaking through my chosen
I'm speaking through my natural world
Just be still

Listen to me
Just listen
I'm always speaking to you
I speak about what I consider relevant
Open your ears
Open your heart
Just be still
Just listen

LOVED

Oh Father

Oh Father
Your love has been consistent and relentless
Your love has caused me to be
Protected at all times
Your love has insulated me against
The flickering flames of fiery trials
Your love has calmed me while I walked through
Uncomfortable valleys
Even the Valley of Death

Oh Father
Your love has fashioned my relationship
With others
Your love has shaped the way I view
Myself
Your love has covered
My multiple mistakes
Your love has taught me
Principles that permeate
Through every thread of my life

Oh Father
Your love has disciplined me when I've
Had not so 'bright' ideas
Your love has guided me through
Important decisions
Your love has healed me when I have
Been sick or hurting
Your love has sustained me when I was
Tired and weak,
Wishing I could just spend some time
Under the juniper tree

Oh Father
I am so grateful for your love
I am really appreciative of your acceptance
I am committed to fulfilling the purpose
That you have designed
With me in mind
Although, it is inadequate in comparison
Father, I just want to say I love you too

My Boys

The tears well up and slowly spill over
As they run down my face
They etch out a memorial
To you my children
Each tear drop paying
Its respects and tribute
Outing the flame of my dreams

You both were full of so much vitality
Loving life, loving music
You both expressed your individuality
By the way you moved, tossed, leapt
Inside me
You had a life I never saw
But yet
A life tangible to me

The enormity of my love for you
Shaped my excitement
Moulded my anticipation
Of lives shared until my death
My vision for you both was huge
I eagerly counted the days and weeks
Until I could hold you

Nurse you
Nurture you

Piercing pain
Piercing screams
Collide
At the news your life was ending
Unable to imagine continuity of my own

My mind, my heart both shattered
Converted into shards of glass
"You'll be able to pick up the pieces and move on"
They said
With little appreciation of the horror of the task

Hazy vision prevents me
From seeing the cloudy fusion
Of milk and tears
Both simultaneously rolling down
A testament to my empty arms
A vibrant reminder that not just my mind
But my body expected you to be there
With me
Warm and snugly
Not cold elsewhere

At your funerals
I stared at your tiny white house

Only I knew
That a chunk of my heart
Was inside that coffin
Buried with you

My Boys
Time has passed
The pain is duller
But my love for you
Remains bright
I often think of you
What could have been
Irreplaceable ones
I miss you dearly

My Beloved Sister

While playing with my dolls alone
I longed for you
To play with you
To speak with you
To share with you

I begged and pleaded for you
Never getting an answer
Year after year
Conscious of my loneliness…..

Just when I gave up hope
I was told you were coming
The excitement and thrill
Spread through each area
Of my limited life
School and Church
I told everyone you were on your way

The call – you're here!
Unspeakable delight
The beginning of a love
So strong it can't be defined
By words or by touch
But yet tangible in the atmosphere

Because of you
I have experienced astonishing pride
Observed remarkable beauty
Understood profoundly dependability
Received unconditional
And unrestrained love

Now almost three decades on
I'm still ecstatic
Incessantly grateful for you
Constantly enjoying
Playing with you
Speaking with you
Sharing with you

Daddy

Daddy you have always
Been there for me
As a child, to provide and protect
As an adult, to share and advise
I love you so much Dad
You have been a constant support

Daddy I know
You have always looked out
For my best interest
Even when we have disagreed
I understand that my independence
Doesn't always allow you to feel needed
And this can sometimes affect
Your sense of purpose

But Dad now you're ageing
Whilst you want to do
I just want you to be
Be what you ask?
Be healthy
Be cognisant

Be stimulated by new opportunities
And events
Be happy
Be there to phone, text or visit

The day is approaching
When your being won't be
For me your purpose now is to take the
Best care of yourself
Body, Mind and Spirit
If you can't do it for you
Then please Dad do it for me

My Strong Warrior

My Strong Warrior
You are feisty and fearless
Your passion captures
All you do and say

Strong Warrior
Your necessity to defend
Gets you in so much
Trouble sometimes
I know there are times
It's hard for you
To understand
How it all turned out
Different to what you expected
But as you grow
Wisdom will teach you the difference
Between shielding and attacking
It will teach you how to be more
Strategic in your warfare

Strong Warrior
It is my constant prayer
That as you mature
You will develop
In your God-given purpose
Seeking God's Kingdom
As you turn into the man
Within whom worship lives

I am honoured to be entrusted with you

Gift of God

My Gift of God
Your brilliance
Shines through
In the way you express
Your creativity and love

So unique and gentle
Your strength radiates from within
You touch so many lives
With your warmth
Unaware of your impact

Your zeal for discussion and debate
Is often misunderstood
But don't let this deter you
You have a voice for a purpose
I'm excited with anticipation
I can't wait to see how
God will use this talent
He has placed within you
To build His Church

Many have marvelled
And been inspired by
Your ability to worship Our Heavenly Father
Unrestrained, untarnished
Its purity and simplicity
Is illuminating

My Gift of God
Continue to love the Lord
And remember
You are not only a gift to me
But also to the world

I am honoured to be entrusted with you

Jacqueline Robinson has been a Christian since childhood. She is a professional manager who lives in London with her two children.

You can contact the author on
jewelmark@hotmail.com

You can purchase a copy of this book at
www.jewelmarkpress.co.uk